REFINED

A Guide to Accept and Release the Things that No Longer Serve You

Chavis D. Walker

The contents of this book, including but not limited to the accuracy of events, people, and places depicted; opinions expressed, and any advice given, or actions are accurate at the time of going to press, and the publisher or author cannot accept responsibility for any errors or omissions, however, caused. No responsibility for the loss or damage to any person acting, or refraining from action, as a result of the material in the publication can be accepted by the editor, publisher, or author.

First Printing

ISBN 9798218003425

Printed in the United States of America

CONTENTS

PREFACE

I used to be embarrassed to be me until God showed me who I was and told me I was chosen.

Now I see with new eyes, through a new lens.

I'm no longer embarrassed about who I am or what I've been through. The good, the bad, and the ugly. What I discovered, which is most important, is the beauty in the journey. I realized that this journey was not only for me but for all those attached to me. It has been the road map to my success. I did something that may seem to be difficult to some. I accepted that I needed Jesus. I was broken. God says in Psalm

51:17 The sacrifice acceptable to God is a broken spirit; a broken and contrite heart, O God, you will not despise.

My reality is I was toxic; I was a victim; I was a mess, I was broken, I was hurt, I was angry. And there is no one to blame. It may sound crazy, but trust me, it's the truth. You may be thinking, momma, daddy, etc., but GOD!

I had to sacrifice my ego and say that I was not ok. I had to hand it over to something bigger than me. To become a better me, I needed to be made new; I needed God to create in me a clean heart. I could not die here. Suffering and brokenness are not my portions. I could no longer hide it! God showed me that brokenness is not the end but the way! Only through my brokenness will I get my breakthrough and be able to break the things that have plagued my family forward. The breaking is in the broken.

This was my first introduction to the Boundary Awareness and Check Point Committee.

They are a part of the Responsibility and Account-ability Association partnered with yours truly, Jesus Christ.

The beauty in being a part of such a take-charge squad is that I GREW.

Now, I'd like to share my gratitude to my faithful fa-ther, God. Thank you, God, for loving me and show-ing me grace and mercy. Thank you for protecting and covering my journey as I've traveled through some hard times, some self-inflicted other times, no fault of my own.

God, thank you, I have been gracefully broken. I now know everything I need is already inside me, and all things are possible. I sit in a posture of surrender.

I ask that you cover, release, and supply the person reading these words. Through this reading, I intend to pierce your eyes with words that will light a fire and refine your spirit so that God can use you and help you achieve the goal of developing and walking into your purpose. The time is NOW; YOUR time is NOW! Allow yourself to become the greatest you that you can be! Today is the day for you to believe in yourself, be honest about who you are, and become accountable for managing your responsibility to become a better human.

I'm living proof that prayer changes things. As my relationship with God has gotten better, all things around me have as well. Better than I could have ever imagined. This guide is not only inspiring but life-changing. If you are finally tired and ready to take charge of your life, here's the way. I won't promise this will happen with ease. I only ask that you allow yourself to be free and choose to unlearn and relearn new habits that will drive you to a place of peace, mentally, emotionally, and spiritually free. Self-care has become the new norm; wow, who knew? No, really, who knew?

If I had known it was ok to love myself more and do other things in moderation, where would I be? I definitely would not have written this book; therefore, there's my hallelujah. The journey to self-care is painfully pleasurable. Once you agree it is ok to be you, I promise it will change your life.

This book will guide you through your acceptance of accountability and teach you how to create permanent positive changes, establish new healthy habits, and love yourself more. This book is intended to hug your spirit and release you from inner spaces, removing barriers and strongholds by beginning to break the chains that we keep on ourselves and don't even realize it. Acknowledging behavior patterns will become the best thing you will ever do for yourself. You will start to experience and bear witness to God's unconditional love. You will be able to testify about his many miracles, signs, and wonders. You will become submerged in God's grace and forgiveness and reap the reward abundantly. Loving yourself is a priority over all things. Never forget that we serve a jealous God. The mission is always to spread the good news of God's glory, but the goal is to walk into your purpose and fulfill his will.

Major favor is upon you.

Be Blessed,
Chavis D. Walker

~

DEDICATION

The Fifth Commandment Exodus 20:2-17 "Honor your father and mother."

Curtis, the man I'm proud to call Dad. My one call, that's all! Thank you for being a stand-up guy—the epitome of what it means not to allow perception to create the narrative. I'm grateful. Wisdom is Wealth and you, my guy, are indeed my angel on earth. Thank you for standing up when you could have walked away, your love superseded the circumstance, and I will be forever grateful.

Daisy M, my Momma, the only one I got! Thank you for always doing your best. Thank you for making every effort to protect me from what I could not understand. Because of you, I am strong, and my love and appreciation for you have grown beyond what I could have imagined. We have navigated some of the most challenging times as mother and daughter, but I know the Father kept us through it all. He allowed us to journey this way to show other mothers and daughters that healing and togetherness are their portions, too. I truly believe this was one of the best lessons of grace, mercy, and forgiveness, but unconditional love is the greatest. I love you, Beautiful. I honor you and appreciate you. Your sacrifice was not in vain, and your teachings did not fall on death's ears. God did it. I now understand. You started saying this to me when I was just a baby, and it will forever be special to me, we now get to share it with others in a book… So, Who do you love? (You) Who do I love? (Me) And what we gotta do? (Stick together) Right on!

To my children, Ajha, Hennessey, and CJ, always know your WHY in life and stay grounded in your why. If you always know your why you will always find your way. You have always been my why. I love you.

And lastly, my amazing and loving husband, Alton. God did a thing, and you are one of many expressions of his unconditional love for me. He knew what I needed, and he sent you. My protector, supporter, confidant, and best friend, Thank you for being the man that God created you to be. Thank you for being so intentional about me. I continue to look forward to tomorrow with you by my side.

ACKNOWLEDGMENTS

To Pamela Sykes, thank you for receiving me with open arms as I journeyed through uncertain times. It allowed me to be present with myself and restore my relationship with God. I'm forever grateful to call you a friend.

To Christina Johnson, thank you for responding that day and extending an invitation to join the room in the Clubhouse app. That was a game-changer, and it unlocked so many things in me. Thank you for your obedience.

Thank you to the Clubhouse morning gratitude space, "The DRIP SQUAD," and the evening Gratitude Room.

To Dr. Pamela Gurley for sharpening me and seeing me through in making this the best and first of many to come. Your passion and your love for writing have inspired me. Your ambition and determination to excel are what motivate me to keep pushing. Thank you for showing me it can be done.

Dr. George Kostakis, I know this will catch you completely by surprise, but there is no way I could leave you out. You will never understand the gratitude I have for you. Thank you for trusting me to manage my responsibilities within the workplace and accomplish my very own goals. Thank you for recognizing and understanding how important it is for me to create my success and make my dreams come true.

INTRODUCTION

So, let's talk about the cover.

There are catchphrases I like to use, and when you read them, you will know.

I will also list definitions that will be extremely important for you to become acquainted with, learn the difference, and quickly discern your behaviors.

Proceed with caution: You will experience spiritual turbulence and may have the desire to cry, scream, or shout. It is highly recommended that you lean into it.

Do not hold back if you need to cry; let it out. That release is a part of your healing journey.

Be unashamed for acknowledging and saying, "thank you, Jesus!" Say it with "yo chess!"

If you feel led to ask God for forgiveness, mean it, be still, and know it is done. He does not require you to repeat it repeatedly -and I promise you that one time is enough. This is the training of exercising your faith muscle.

Know that it is already done, give it to him, and take your hands off it. Leave it where you lay it. Laying your burdens down is a real thing.

There is only one thing required of you while you navigate this read.

I want you to read Romans chapter 5: verses 1-11:

5 Therefore, since we have been justified through faith, we have peace with God through our Lord Jesus Christ, 2 through whom we have gained access by faith into this grace in which we now stand. And we boast in the hope of the glory of God. 3 Not only so, but we also glory in our sufferings because we know that suffering produces perseverance; 4 perseverance, character; and character, hope. 5 And hope does not put us to shame because God's love has been poured into our hearts through the Holy Spirit, who has given us.

6 You see, at just the right time, when we were still powerless, Christ died for the ungodly. 7 Very rarely will anyone die for a righteous person, though for a good person, someone might possibly dare to die. 8 But God demonstrates his love for us in this: While we were still sinners, Christ died for us.

9 Since his blood has now justified us, how much more shall we be saved from God's wrath through him! 10 For if, while we were God's enemies, we were reconciled to him through the death of his Son, how much more, having been reconciled, shall we be saved through his life! 11 Not only is this so, but we also boast in God through our Lord Jesus Christ, through whom we have now received reconciliation."

EXTEND YOURSELF SOME GRACE!

WHEN YOU KNOW BETTER, IT'S YOUR RESPONSIBILITY TO TAKE CHARGE OF YOUR LIFE AND DO BETTER!

No one can judge you; no one has to know that you are navigating this level of healing.

This is your guide to freedom.

This is your portal to access forgiveness within. Before we get started, say out loud,

"I forgive myself."

Come on, say it like you mean it!

I forgive myself!

I acknowledge and accept my participation in some of the things that have plagued me, and I forgive myself.

I realize that some of my choices have caused me to stumble, and I forgive myself.

I accept responsibility for my life and will take full accountability for my life moving forward. When I don't get it right, I will be quick to extend grace and FORGIVE MYSELF.

Nothing after today matters.

I AM FORGIVEN!

Now let's get into it and why I chose the title "Refined."

I believe Refined and Accountability go together. I like to say grow together because some things won't happen overnight and need time to manifest.

But there were some words - "hard truths" - that I had to tell myself to be healed and free my children and grandchildren from generational curses.

It's easy to find a word to address what's been crippling our growth if we allow ourselves to be HONEST. DON'T forget that real is the new fake; you must tell yourself the truth.

You can't truly make changes until you admit that there is a problem.

There is only one person on this planet that you can't lie to, and that's you.

You will always know the truth about yourself.

There's a truth that is connected to you forever. This is where the generational curses are birthed and spill over onto our children, grandchildren, and the many generations to come. We must be mindful of the things that stunt our growth and hinder us from being of good character; we must take control of the narrative.

Always remember beyond your faults and extend yourself some GRACE, MERCY, and FORGIVE-NESS. You're not the worst person in the world and won't be the last to make mistakes. Because of others, we may fall into a sunken place, and it is our responsibility not to stay stuck there. We have more power than we tend to know.

Everyone has crosses to bear; it's a sin that humans cannot weigh.

When you know better, you simply have to do better. I know this may seem difficult when all you know how to be is who you are now.

Your mindset and state of being will be the only thing that ever truly matters if you adjust your posture and expect the absolute best of yourself, NOT OTHERS. You must not host any level of expectation from humans because we always disappoint and hurt one another. This is why grace is so important. We are all learning to become the best versions of ourselves, which will not always look like what others think they should be. The priority is and should always be you.

The better you feel about yourself, the more productive you will be and the more productive you become. It will have a positive influence on all of those connected to you. Everything requires a response, and it's a natural chain reaction.

We spend countless hours and years on the hamster wheel in ridiculous, redundant cycles attempting to unlock success as if it's magic. The only thing that's missing is accountability.

Accept the responsibility for your very own accountability!

How you show up for yourself reflects the abundance you inherit here on earth. Do not continue to pour from an empty cup.

I am going to share with you what I call my alphabet journey. I call it the alphabet journey because I developed an exercise that helped me identify root issues that kept me in stuck places. With each letter in the alphabet, I searched a word in the dictionary to ensure that it was a fit. It's important to know the words we use because there is power in our words.

It took great courage for me to show up and think I could write a book, especially hosting such delicate afflictions. After all the hurt, pain, disappointment, rejection, and sorrow I've endured over the years, it made me think I was just some worthless being that was here taking up space. But my Abba father grabbed hold of me and told me I was uniquely designed to fulfill a purpose. He was intentional when he created me and created me in his image. It was him that granted me my first breath, he walked with me, and he is my friend. That, to me, is amazing. Romans 8:31: "If God be for us, who can be against us."

It's time that we stop using our pain as a crutch. It's time we stop using the brokenness as the storyline for empathy and make our pain point our paying point. Allow your story to become your power move.

We have taken our ability to charm others, manipulate and then find ourselves believing our own mess.

I accepted in my twenties that I was a habitual liar, and I needed to understand why

Habitual means …..

I made it a habit to lie to survive. This is not something I came up with. I inherited the behavior; I witnessed it happen all around me. I also noticed that people accept and become okay with the behavior.

So, let's think about this for a moment; if the examples around us show us that certain toxic behaviors are ok -, this simply is the rebirthing of generational curses.

This is why it is essential to focus on being honest and not REAL.

There is a difference, ya know.

Real - relating to something as it is and not as it may be

Honest - free of deceit and untruthfulness: sincere

Now let me break this all the way down for you.

You can be real and speak the language, yet your actions don't reflect what you say.

Now here's the thing, it may appear to others that what you speak is indeed your real life.

But at home, where no one can see you, there's no one to bear witness to the things you might be struggling with.

Succumb - fail to resist pressure, temptation, or some other opposing force

Understand this, no, no one is perfect. God doesn't choose perfect people.

If you are reading this book, be confident that you have been chosen.

It took great courage to reveal the most private and sensitive things I have overcome on my journey, BUT I am more than a conqueror, and I was able to overcome my fear of judgment through my ability, to be honest.

BUT- used to introduce a phrase or clause contrasting what was already said or mentioned

The more I spoke in truth and transparency I gained strength, and that strength led to a revelation.

Although this has been my journey, I know I'm not the only one.

Let's not forget this critical factor; there is always a ME TOO.

Me too- someone who will testify that they have shared or witnessed the same experiences you have.

See, you're not alone. I bet you've already had a memory of someone saying, "me too."

I'll even bet you that it was recent.

When we are ready to accept that we need to make changes, we seek resources, including motivational speakers, conferences, self-help books, journals, courses, and the list goes on. There is absolutely nothing wrong with that because this means we are recognizing that we need to make some changes.

We rarely stand in the mirror and say to ourselves, "you need to get your shit together." And we need to. This is also speaking into ourselves. Don't appease yourself by always saying what you want to hear; you must also be assertive.

Don't be surprised if you catch a cuss word here or there.

I'm intentional about navigating differently, but I want to encourage you to accept that we are human and not expected to always get it right.

I'm unashamed to say that I've lived! I've been a tequila and whiskey weekend warrior. I've been the model club hopper. I still enjoy a groovy day party and dancing. I've indulged a great deal in partying like a rockstar. I regret nothing.

However, I will be the first to say THANK YOU, GOD, FOR SAVING A WRETCH LIKE ME! I don't deserve to live, but through God, I live on, blessed with a new day to attempt to get it right.

And in my imperfect nature, receive his unlimited grace and mercy, relentless favor and forgiveness, and unconditional love!

Woooooo, ain't he good! My God!

Ok, ok, that was a praise break.

Relentless- Never ending.

Unconditional- despite: not subject to conditions.

To break redundant cycles and generational curses, it is vital to get grounded and rebuild on a solid emotional foundation to break repetitious cycles and generational curses.

You must understand that the word of God will carry you the rest of the way.

I will list a few scriptures that have carried me over and helped me get my mind right.

I'm a mood person, and it changes often.

It can go from praise and worship to trap music, house music, reggae, jazz, soundscapes, and meditation.

Depending on how the wind is blowing and the spaces I'm navigating internally.

I have now set the tone of what to expect.

What I did not say is what NOT to expect, and that is PERFECTION.

You may read this book and say, "what in the hell is this woman talking about," and disagree with every word written. If that's the case, keep your opinion to yourself and pass it on to someone else who may need it.

Opinion- a view or judgment formed about something, not necessarily based on fact or knowledge.

We all have one, and we have the right to it.

We also have the right to respectfully shut the hell up and stop forcing it on others. Forcing someone to accept our views and opinions is a toxic trait. Have you ever met someone that got mad at you because you didn't agree with them about something?

We need to learn how to PEOPLE differently and know the difference between healthy and toxic dialogue.

We can sometimes become so critical in our thoughts. These thoughts are triggered by negative emotions -, whether it be jealousy, envy, or because we are having a hard time accepting and celebrating the success of others anyway., Whatever... you get the picture.

We must learn how to share positive dialogue focusing on the celebration of effort, influenced by encouragement, knowledge, and the sharing of resources to help others become better - IRON SHARPENING IRON.

Instead of selfish perspectives, inject emotional viruses that show up in mindless gossip and crippling rumors.

Crippling rumors- demeaning conversations that host no value and seek ruin in the reputation of another: can cause one to have an emotional setback that can lead to depression, addiction, or even suicide.

Treating people how you want to be treated is a real thing.

REAL-ationships are reflections of UNCONDITIONAL LOVE.

1 Corinthians 13:4-

INTRO TO ALPHA'S

When I was in elementary school and became introduced to writing poems like "A is for amazing just like you," it was always so much fun for me. I also am a big fan of looking up words in the dictionary. I love pairing words with the alphabet. I believe that not only does it teach you new words, but it teaches you what each of them means. While healing my inner child, I did this exercise often and came up with my core Alphas. These are all areas that I had to master to become a better version of myself. As I am still navigating life, I remain a constant work in progress. Let's get started.

ALPHA 1

ATTITUDE

1 Attitude -a settled way of thinking or feeling about someone or something, typically reflected in a person's behavior.

Your attitude is proof positive of what will and won't happen

Your outlook on life is what shapes your outcomes

Perception is NOT everything; as a matter of fact, what we see is not what it is most of the time. Think about it we take the best photos in our good clothes and have an amazing background; to others, we are living our best life, but the reality is or could be that we are hanging on by a thread and ready to just be over it already.

Life indeed is what you make it, but no one said it would be easy. Anything worth having is worth working for. I did not say fight; I do not want one single person assuming that it is healthy to fight over that person, place, or thing that God could be trying to move you from and remove from you.

You must know that despite what things look or feel like, it is all working together for our good

Romans 8:28

Don't be easily taunted or distracted by what you see and feel but be still and KNOW.

Psalm 46:10

It is crucial to have a positive mindset and optimistic thinking habits -; this will curve the appetite to entertain drama.

It will also discourage others from bringing drama to you, creating boundaries.

You will see that the good will always outweigh the bad. Never forget that you have full control and complete authority to change your narrative. The incredible thing about life is that God filled us with purpose, and every day we open our eyes is a new opportunity to try again. Every day is a new day, which means we can start over at any point and time. You can start over as many times as you'd like.

Nothing beats a failure but a try, and as long as you try, you are not failing.

1. What will you do today to change your tomorrow?

2. What or who can keep you from doing it?

3. What will you need to do to achieve what you would like to accomplish?

ALPHA 2

BEHAVIOR AND BOUNDARIES

I had to acknowledge that my behavior was toxic. There is a difference between being charismatic and full of shit.

Full of charm, beautiful, intelligent, BUT conning (persuade (someone) to do or believe something, typically by use of deception.)

Let's keep it ALL THE WAY 100%.

Honestly, that's the only way we will be able to kick it beyond this point.

Everyone has lied or manipulated someone or something to control the outcome of a situation.

And please don't show up with the speech of "well, my intentions were good."

Just STOP IT! Don't give yourself an excuse to show up raggedy.

Remember, it's always important to know your WHY.

Once I stopped refusing to accept the truth about myself, I had to dig deep within to discover why I was motivated to be deceptive.

This brought about some harsh realities. I went through the emotions of being hurt, angry, disappointed, disgusted, and even lonely.

I lost trust in people; hell, I even stopped trusting myself.

I got help!!!! Help!!!!

Let me encourage you to do the best thing in life there is ever to do.

Don't sleep on this information.

GET HELP!

SEEK COUNSELING! FIND SOMEONE THAT YOU CAN TALK TO. Someone who hosts no bias and can hold you accountable. Not your friend that offers sound advice but can't advise his or herself. Not the cousin who appears to have her life in order but is a hot mess when managing her feelings and emotions. AND DEFINITELY not the friend that gives the best relationship advice but is single and rebukes love.

Right here, right now, I want you to FORGIVE YOURSELF! Don't feel bad, ME, TOO!

You're not alone. Guess what? You don't know what you don't know.

And when you know what you know, and it's the wrong information, you can't allow guilt to hold you, hostage, for thinking you knew because you didn't.

It's not your fault. It can take forever to undo what was done, but it can be done and will be done if you make an effort to be better and do better.

Now drink a full 8oz glass of room temperature water so you can prepare your body to release these toxins. I told you earlier that you've been full of shit.

This part here is precisely what it is …. behavior.

We've acknowledged it and are far from done, but let's get into boundaries now.

(: a line that marks limits, a dividing line.).

Let's talk about how boundaries complement destructive behaviors and encourage the birthing of new behaviors.

Once you acknowledge that you are responsible for how you show up and begin to understand cause and effect, You realize it is essential to change your narrative. And what did we say .... It starts with who? You! That's right.

Many of us weren't taught how to love ourselves appropriately. Our parents did what they knew to do and shared it with us.

Most of them didn't know how to show up, nor did they have boundaries, or just maybe due to circumstances, they submitted to their current situations and endured and carried on like good soldiers because they felt there was no way out.

It is important not to repeat these behavior patterns and create boundaries that will keep us in check.

Cause and effect … If you dish it, you need to be able to receive it. What you sow into the ground you must reap a full harvest.

You do not need to be accepting of another person's malicious behavior and their inability to show up better. Offer grace and guard your space. It should always be a priority to protect your peace. But you can't have this attitude and create confrontation and bad energy everywhere you go.

Be the change you want to see in people.

If real love is what you seek, be relentless in offering love freely and never regret it, even when the results you wish don't come to pass. The way God protects us is beyond fathomable.

He's omnipresent; he sees what we can't and knows what we don't.

Trust him always.

Once you have come to terms with who you are, decide what's imperative to be better and embrace change.

Once you do this, you will need to comprehend and accept the following statement fully:

"People are going to leave you. Some of your relationships are going to dissipate."

Yeah, I know it's crazy, right!… You're probably asking yourself why that would happen when I'm being intentional about becoming a better version of myself.

It's simple., Some people are not ready to grow, and everybody can't go where you are going.

God speed

It's ok. Let them go.; Allow the season to change and do not resist. Remember, GOD is Omnipresent. "All things work together for our good."

Offer your well- wishes, say a prayer, and keep it moving.

Respect and appreciate what God is doing and say, "THANK YOU."

We are not responsible for forcing others to grow with us. Give God his children back.

People are NOT our responsibilities. We can offer support and information and move on.

Have you ever heard the saying: You can lead the horse to the water, but you can't make him drink?

Indeed, you cannot make people do what they don't want, nor can you force people to go where you are going.

Therefore, you have to be ok leaving them behind. Release yourself from the pressure of trying to control the uncontrollable and forgive people. We all get it wrong until we get it right.

This prayer was intended to align us with God's word and his way:

"God grant me the serenity to accept the things I cannot change, The courage to change the things I can, And the wisdom to know the difference."

Accept this next assignment with love.

The Serenity Prayer -

Read it, Learn it, and Discern it.

It will surely help you learn how to take your hands off things that don't belong to you.

Some things are not your battles to fight or win – they belong to the Lord.

Things that do not compliment your new narrative and no longer serve you.

Release it.

ALPHA 3

CHARACTER AND CRITICISM

Be of good courage and host good character, but who can genuinely say you host good character? Who's the judge? After all, there is good in all of us.

People everywhere can be so critical of others.

Quick to make an assumption based on what they think they know about you or something that someone else may have said and shared at their level of understanding, which can tentatively not be very much, if I'm honest. After all, anyone with good character should not be creating an act of assassination against another.

Needless to say, these are the ones that are usually guilty as charged.

This is going to be short.

There is only one judge, and this judge is above the law.

Matthew 7:1-2

7 "Do not judge, or you too will be judged.

2 For in the same way you judge others, you will be judged, and with the measure you use, it will be measured to you."

Remember, the way of life is written; when you act according to the word, you can't get it wrong.

That's all.

ALPHA 4

DESPERATION AND DISCIPLINE

It is so easy to get caught in sticky situations. We can make one wrong decision out of desperation, and it will cause an array of other things to take a turn for the worst. This is what makes boundaries so important. Respecting your limitations will prevent you from stepping out of bounds. Don't do things out of desperation. When has a desperate move shown itself fruitful? Usually, a sacrifice was made that jeopardized more than it was worth, which led to regret. I am so guilty of making desperate moves;

although it is true I accomplished what I was seek-ing, I paid a much higher price for it. I robbed myself of my peace, time, and even body.

Desperation will cause you to seek sources that were in seasons that have already ended. Next thing you know, you find yourself in a position you didn't desire to be in, blowing life back into what was dead. We tend to fall into the trap of things and people that are familiar, because familiarity can be comfortable. BUT we have to grow up and leave childish things behind.

Growth is uncomfortable. Who just chooses to be uncomfortable? Growth is necessary. We must learn to endure growing pains so we can level up to the next chapters awaiting our arrival. Going backwards is not growth. The things behind us no longer com-plement our forward progress. When I was in middle school, I wore size five shoes. Now that I'm 41, I wear a 7.5 if. If I attempted to squeeze my foot into a 5, I would be in pain. Depending on the make of the shoe, I could probably get the shoe on my foot, but it doesn't fit. The moment I attempt to walk, it will probably take me out! Why do we constantly find ourselves trying to fit narratives that have hurt us or can cause us a great deal of pain? Accept that you no longer fit, and it's time to go up a size. I don't know about you, but I desire to be comfortable, and being happy is comfortable for me.

It takes great intentions to become disciplined and accept what's needed to align with healthy living. Making a decision that you want more out of life and recognizing that you are full of purpose makes it easier to see the bigger picture. Once you see it, you accept it and must accept that you will be required to show up differently to attain the next level. No matter how hard it gets and how far out of reach it may appear, I promise you it's closer than you think. All you have to do is think you can do it and try! Stand up and tell yourself NO `to the things you need to say no to. If they are out of alignment with the things you desire to accomplish, you must learn to respect your boundaries. When you respect your very own boundaries, others will as well.

ALPHA 5

EGO EFFORT AND ELEVATION

When you are intentional about changing your narrative and desire to heal, you CAN NOT HOST EGO!

Ego and pride are the pathways to a great demise.

Ego will ruin relationships not only with others but with yourself.

Now let's pause for a second and recognize Beyonce says, "she has a big ego."

But she can back it up!

Take a second and think about what that means.

Now we don't know precisely what that means for her and how it applies to her life but what I know is feeding your ego when you cannot be humble, amongst other things, is a failure.

Ask yourself these questions:

Are you humble enough to apologize even when you don't think you're wrong?

How often do you debate with someone about how you may have made them feel?

We cannot debate with others about how they reflect on how we have made them feel.

An apology is necessary if someone tells you that you hurt their feelings.

You might have been 100% correct with what you said, and even saying it with the sweetest tone does not change the fact that it hurt them.

Consider this information as the cutting board; we are far from done.

Acknowledging how you make people feel is essential.

But you can't ride the conviction wheel until it falls off

Some of us focus on keeping it real and cannot deliver feedback with tactfulness. Keeping it real does not require it to be delivered with harsh words.

Love protects with correction, yet delivery is crucial.

Practicing mindfulness will provide essential coaching on how you treat yourself and others.

Making every effort to practice mindfulness will push the inside elevation button, and you will find yourself rising above all things that no longer serve you.

Letting go of ego and making every effort to become a better you will elevate you beyond what you could have imagined. Now prepare to leap into your next. Humbled and hungry to grow.

You have to want to be a good person.

Let's keep it pushing.

Say it with me:

"I Forgive myself, and I have Faith that I am Forgiven."

ALPHA 6

~

FORGIVENESS

Forgiving someone is not just for them; it's also for you; staying mad and holding grudges is like causing a delay in traffic. We can't move forward when we are sitting in unforgiveness. Do not get caught in the rapture of being stuck in unforgiveness; it has too much power and control. Have you ever been out somewhere having a grand ole time, and someone that wronged you entered the room, and you find yourself suddenly uncomfortable and are instantly pissed off all over again? Now the fun that you were having has taken a backseat to bullshit. And maybe you still try to rise to the occasion and pretend to be unbothered, but it's a fact that you're thinking about it? Yeah, NOPE, this cannot continue to be your portion. You control the narrative, and you control how things affect you. Forgive and let go. You cannot harbor ill feelings in the places God wants to dwell in your life. I did not say forget how someone treated you. I did not say you have to interact. God forgives us and if he can forgive us for the things that he knows about us, make it an easy task for you to host the same heart.

ALPHA 7

∾

GRATITUDE

If I never learn anything for the remainder of my time on this place that we call earth, I am most grateful that I have learned what it truly means to be grateful for everything.

Having an attitude of gratitude indeed causes a response from God.

When you are grateful and appreciate what you have it increases your chances of receiving more if that's what you desire. Too often we take life and what we do have for granted.

You don't have to believe me, but it's true. After all, I'm just a nobody trying to tell everybody about somebody who saves, someone who forgives when you know you're wrong, and somebody who offers grace and mercy when you're the least deserving.

It's really simple. All you have to do is say, "thank you, Jesus, and your life right now will take a complete shift!" A turn for the better.

If you're exhausted with the hamster wheel of poverty, lack, hurt feelings, broken hearts, voids and loneliness, Right now, I dare you to say the name Jesus and have an expectation that he is about to take complete control and help you to change your narrative.

Don't be embarrassed or ashamed, remember. Remember to "Say it with your chest!" Do it with me and say it loud, "THANK YOU, JESUS! I'm grateful for all that you have done and all that you are doing with me, for me, and through me."

The only thing God wants us to do is to acknowledge him in all things, everything; everything after that is history.

Say thank you, your abundance awaits.

Oh wait, just one more thing, here's a little secret I need to tell you.

Everything attached to me wins, so just know, you, yes, you ARE WINNING!

Connectivity is real.

He is doing it for me, which means he's doing it for you, and everyone connected to you.

Put on your seatbelt and prepare for take-off.

You will experience some shaking because the enemy is now aware that you are awake. You are preparing to embrace the shift in the atmosphere. Rebuke the distractions. God wants us to trust him so he can trust us with more. Be still and stand on what you know!

Trust him, for all things work together for the good of the Lord!

Romans 8:28

ALPHA 8

❧

HONESTY

Y'all, sometimes being honest can be hard, and now that I know what I know, here is a fun fact that I'd like to share.

Everyone in the world tells at least one lie a day.

It doesn't matter who you are or your title or profession; you lie.

Some forms of lying include exaggerating and stretching the truth, withholding information, delivering misinformation, or creating false narratives.

Let's talk about creating a false narrative.

If you are in your head and coming up with your very own conclusions, whether they are common sense conclusions or not.

The fact of the matter is that it is an ASSUMPTION.

Unless you have hard-core facts about something, it creates a false narrative if you deliver information based on your opinion or feelings on how it should go.

Do you see how this behavior is why it's a lie?

Meanwhile, if you don't know something, don't attempt to share just to be part of a conversation. It is ok to be a listener. Personally, I enjoy listening more than sharing., You learn so much more when you absorb what's being shared. You learn a lot more about people when you allow them to talk.

People will tell you exactly who they are if you just listen. You don't always have to be heard.

Speak and share when it's necessary. This is called picking and choosing your battles wisely. Every battle is not yours, and every debate does not require you to become a great debater. However, I encourage you that when it's your time to speak, STAND IN YOUR POWER, SPEAK WITH POWER, know your stuff, and have facts to back it up.

I always tell people they have to learn how to fight right. Know why you are talking about it. Here we go, here we go. "Beyoncé, I talk like this 'cause I can back it up; I got a big egoooo, such a big egoooo."

(That's me singing, y'all.)

See that ….. talk yo shit, B (JayZ).

I'm such a big fan of the Carters (if you haven't noticed by now).

I pray that you get it, but if you don't, feel free to type www.thesynergyhouse.com and register for The Accountability Corner Coaching course., Allow me to help you shift your mindset and step into your power. I can show you how to replace old negative thinking habits with new practices that create permanent positive changes.

If you'd like to understand more and need one-on-one time with me, you can contact me by email at bysynergyhouse@gmail.com.

ALPHA 9

~

INCOMPLETE

Have you ever overpromised, over-committed, and under-delivered?

Don't be too quick to respond because you may end up telling a lie.

Even if you got it done in the final hour, you know it could've been better had you planned properly and given yourself more time, right?

Well, guess what? I used to do this silly shit all the time, so don't feel bad. Give yourself some grace but be mindful of this; now that we've announced this behavior and called it out, you can no longer give yourself an excuse to keep showing up with poor mismanagement of time.

Time is valuable, time is currency. You can no longer throw your money away.

You can no longer show up as if tomorrow is waiting on you.

You now understand seizing the moment and expounding on opportunities as they present themselves.

You don't have to get ready if you stay ready.

Completion has to happen. It's no longer optional.

Get your portion! Success is your portion!

Everything you want, you have to work for it. But I tell you, work your prayer life and watch God work for you.

Don't allow the things you consider imperfections distract you from knowing that God created you and loves you just the way you are. He sees what you see as ugly scars as beautiful markings to remind you of how far you've come and celebrate where you're headed.

ALPHA 10

JUDGMENT AND JUSTIFIED

You and your justified judgment

Get out of here! Who have we ever thought we were to judge someone based on what we think we know - whether right or wrong. Right there, I want you to lean into it, whether right or wrong.

Let me explain. I am great at problem-solving and discovering solutions to things that some people struggle with. My thoughts of how things should go could be right, yet this does not grant authority for me to apply pressure on someone to live a certain way and be different. I learned this by being a mom and giving my mom hell. Yeah, I said that. (Momma, I'm sorry, I know now that you were only trying to protect me from what I couldn't see.)

Thank you, Father God, for your grace, mercy, and forgiveness. I forgive myself.

We want to have control so badly that we will emotionally manipulate from a place of judgment. Have you ever said that you loved someone and the moment they make what appears and may even be apparent a bad decision and end up talking to someone that may show up as a "friend" about that person, but "I love you has lived on your lips for the longest time for them?

How have you loved them to such depth, and you speak with such judgment about them. You have a strong opinion about how someone else should live their life.

Ask yourself, do you follow your advice? Do you practice what you preach? Do you walk it like you talk it?

I digress.

Be sure to focus on yourself, your healing, your wants, your needs, your choices, and your commitments. Give God his children back; it's not your business. Pray for people and their healing and their protection.

Don't shoot the messenger; love corrects.

ALPHA 11

∿

KNOWLEDGE

Knowledge is POWER. You dominate the world by placing a book in your hands.

There is so much history and wisdom in books.

Being able to read is a privilege to some folks, and others just take this amazing gift for granted and don't even try it. You could say that this is judgmental. But Love corrects! I want you to be great. I want you to connect the WHY behind this reading, go back to the title and rest assured that this is the level of knowledge and guidance you need to move with good intentions.

It is important to feed your mind with things worth taking up space in your head.

Instead of being so quick to say how much you don't like to read, take control, and begin to tell yourself how much you enjoy it.

Just as we can talk ourselves out of things, we have the same ability to talk ourselves into things.

Begin to take charge and change the narrative right here today.

Talk yourself out of doing things that take up space and bear no fruit; instead, talk yourself into doing something that will serve you forward, grow your intellect, and increase your wisdom.

Your earthly inheritance awaits you.

Books encourage you to discover more of your purpose. The power you need is already inside you; it's waiting to be activated.

Come alive, insides, come alive.

ALPHA 12

~

LYING AND LOVE

Have you ever felt disappointed with love?

Have you ever felt that love let you down?

Have you ever said to yourself that enough is enough?

Better yet, have you ever felt that enough was enough, yet you would not respect the expiration date and thought maybe, just maybe, things would change, and they never did.

What if I told you that you're the problem?

What if I told you that the moment you choose yourself and prioritize yourself, you would begin to draw in more of what serves you than just calling in and allowing the subconscious nonnegotiable to take up space.

By now, we have all heard the saying:

"You must do something different to get different results."

Well, it's true.

Unclosed chapters and a lack of boundaries keep us incarcerated and in bondage.

I like to call it the hamster wheel.

Have you ever seen a hamster on a hamster wheel? If not, Google is the same as walking on a treadmill; you're not going anywhere. Oddly enough, there is motion. But if it's not elevating you and stimulating you enough to want more, what's the real purpose of opting into going nowhere fast.

How long will it take before accepting ownership of our choices reflects what we allow.

We ignore red flags with the ideology that we are capable of changing others when the truth is that's just simply not our portion. We emotionally manipulate ourselves into believing that just if we ….. things will change and be different.

Well, reflect on just how far hosting this idea has gotten you

Did it change? And if it did good for you but was it you that made it change, or did you inspire the change? There is a difference. And if you inspired the change, good for you.

I celebrate for you and with you, but the fact remains that you were required to take action and ownership of the flow, and it is a response to what you allowed or didn't allow.

You are the author. Will you continue to write the same script and switch characters, or will you change the narrative, create healthy boundaries, and hold yourself accountable.

You can't love anyone more than you love yourself. You can't care more for others than you care for yourself. Learn to be kind to yourself, learn to respect yourself, and learn to honor yourself. Speak life Into yourself.

You're worthy, you're powerful, you're loved, and you're forgiven.

ALPHA 13

MISTAKES AND MOTIVES

Accepting Accountability for our actions can be extremely difficult to do. Standing in the mirror and accepting what we see can be even harder, but do you know what's even harder? Recognizing that these things are an issue.

We stay in sunken spaces so long that it becomes the norm, and when others tell us that we are there, we can quickly become offended because we can't accept what we hear.

Hearing things about ourselves can come across like judgment; however, it's not always the case.

We have all endured some bad times and have seen some dark days. If you disagree, I'm curious why you have continued to read this far. Whatever your reason may be, God bless you. Perhaps you are in denial and need a friend. No matter the reason, I love you.

Ok, back to business.

I am guilty of waddling in my mess. I am guilty of making mistakes. I am guilty of pretending that my actions were mistakes and were indeed intentional, aka motive.

Again, recognizing and owning behavior, accepting accountability

I want to soften the message here because this one is very delicate and still, to this very day, triggers some things for me.

When you notice your shoe is untied, you instantly want to bend down to tie it so that you won't trip and fall.

To do any of the above things I mentioned, there's something critical in the process, like learning how to tie a shoe. Before seeking a solution, you must identify it and understand the why.

Do you remember earlier what I said … Always know your Why

My why keeps me pushing forward

Having friends, make more money, receive love, gain opportunities, etc., but they have not always worked in my favor. Delay is not denial, and rejection is God's protection. It could even be that what we want is not as big as what God wants us to have.

Now when I reflect on my journey, where I've been, the people I've encountered, and the many things that I've overcome and even achieved, I instantly remember the disappointment, the hurt, and the pain that has come along with it. It's heartbreaking! But my God…. I began to hear someone say to make your pain point your paying point.

All of this has caused some deeply rooted emotional scars.

But the word of the Lord says

"All things work together for good to them that love God, to them who are the called according to his purpose". Romans 8:28.

I've learned to be grateful for every emotional milestone; achieving is believing that I can do all things through Christ who strengthens me.

Philippians 4:13

Right at this moment, I'm meditating and writing while listening to the beautiful, talented, and super gifted artist **Geminelle's album Mantra Loops, Volume 1 song Everything I need**

She knows just what to say to help drive the divine flow within.

You should try it. Let's get back on track.

Please don't sit and ponder on your inability to be a perfect human. God sacrificed his only son so we wouldn't have to endure prolonged suffering. He also wanted us to experience his mighty works and wonders; therefore, he didn't choose a perfect soul.

We are chosen. Our lives mean something. We are warriors, healers, and doctors. We are love. We are everything that we want to be. We are more than enough. Nothing is by chance, and there is no such thing as coincidence. God has us right where we are supposed to be. Let him continue to do a mighty work in you.

What he has for us is greater and much bigger than we could ever imagine for ourselves.

We deserve it, and besides, it's our birthright.

ALPHA 14

NO

No is a complete sentence.

No helps to encourage healthy boundaries and get rid of the toxic shit that's attached to many things. Take your power back! Say no!

Stop sacrificing what you can't see to be a people pleaser.

Stop giving away what you don't have. Giving away what you do have to doesn't respect or value you. Yeah, No! We are releasing what no longer serves us.

Forgive forward.

You must protect your peace. Release yourself from feeling obligated to help when you don't have one. Say no to the invitation to a party when you know your body needs rest. I think you can catch my drift.

You first

ALPHA 15

~

OPPORTUNIST

They say you should exercise every opportunity to glow up, come up, move up, you get my drift.

But what if it's at the expense of someone else's heart?

Have you ever run game on someone? Have you ever played someone?

Have you ever convinced someone of something and told them you felt a way and you really didn't, but the gain of being misleading was in your favor?

Big ups to you if you haven't; I have.

There were times I walked away disappointed in myself for being a user, and other times I didn't give a damn.

You know, we humans find a way to validate our behavior and will believe that we had good cause to ignore our moral compass.

I want to let you know that owning your mess does not release you from the karmic response that the universe will give back to you. You will get back what was sown.

Boy, have I experienced some turbulent times. I remember clearly how sometimes things felt trying, and I would instantly reflect on a time when I did not show up in good character.

It doesn't require me to be specific here; just know that I have endured my seasons on the raft, and I'm still grateful.

I read a scripture today that gave me knowledge and understanding of God's word for loaning and borrowing money.

What an eye-opener it was. Luke 6:27-38. I won't put it here, but I expect you to be intentional about reading it.

Even if you haven't picked your Bible up in years, do it today. This scripture will change your life and perception if you allow it.

Besides, you've made it this far; you should just do it now. I can wait.

....

....

....

So, what do you think? Wasn't that like WOW!

Say what?! It's a sin to loan money and ask for it back. I almost felt free of some debts I had out there, but I had a gentle reminder that good character is the key, and to be of good character, you have to be a keeper of your word.

I struggled at every age, and my relationship with money has been terrible. Unfortunately, I inherited it; I definitely didn't choose it or ask for it to be this way. From credit struggles to rob Peter to pay Paul, borrowing from this person, over-promising to piece it together, and lacking the next payday because there just isn't enough.

I raised three 3kids involuntarily and alone due to divorce and never being able to see things the same.

Lacking the necessary support often had my back against the wall. I couldn't call family, and no one could or would help me. I might add that I am always stretched thin, people-pleasing, and making that shit look easy. Thank you, Father. I don't look anything like what I've been through!

My hallelujah belongs to you, God!!! THANK YOU, JESUS!

It could've been worse, so much worse………

I'm back …

I was never taught the importance of being financially literate. My environment showed me it was cool to move when you couldn't pay the rent, good credit was for white people, and put the lights and gas in your child's name when you ruin your relationship with the utility companies.

Here I am, 38 addresses later, having acquired most of them before I turned 25.

My momma did the best she could with what she knew and what she had.

(Mommy, I love you, thank you for always doing your best.)

Let's pause

Round of applause for those parents that didn't know what to do but still got it done.

I'm not complaining about my journey; I'm celebrating my ability to rise above it.

Now that I know better, I choose to be better.

Shall we ….

Here we are, the opportunist recognizing what's kept me from prospering and gaining financial momentum and wealth without all the suffering. Accepting that this was a mess before I was born, realizing that this ain't livin.

Here's the other part of the mess: I was overcompensating for my children's father not being present.

I desired to do so much more than required because of his absence.

All I can do is shake my head now, but I have no regrets.

These things wedged together helped me draw an honest conclusion about myself.

My relationship with money was doomed from the beginning.

With all these things being problematic, My God always sent an Angel. There was always a ram in the bush.

I'm purposely spending a great deal of time on this topic because I'm still addressing my mishandling of a few people.

If I could change it, I would. But even in that, I'm grateful that they were sent, I'm grateful that they said yes, I'm grateful that a seed was sown, and gracefully the narrative in my life has changed, and things are in alignment.

Lying, embellishing truths, spinning narratives, and manipulating to get the desired outcome that works in your interest is the example of an opportunist.

It's foul, and nothing good comes of it. It might appear as if you came up, but truthfully you dig a hole for yourself, and it will require more than a shovel to dig your way out.

Right here, right now.

Forgive yourself for finding a way to survive; it wasn't the best or the most honest way.

This is why I believe it to be true that God is always continually working to care for us, even when we aren't talking to him. That's that mercy, grace, and forgiveness. Another example of his unconditional love is that despite my despicable behavior, he still chose me.

Please, whatever you do, learn to take complete charge of your life; accountability will not always be the easiest assignment to navigate, but I promise it gets easier with time.

Be of good character, learn to keep your word, and don't go seeking selfish advantages; they may indeed harm others or put them at risk.

Also, sometimes it's good to go back and right your wrongs; other times, it's best to let sleeping dogs stay asleep.

Either way, have those intimate conversations with God. Be open and honest about everything - he already knows he's your best friend and confidant. If you can't keep it real with anyone else, I promise you can keep it real with Him. Keep talking; he speaks back.

Look for his many miracles, signs, and wonders. They are all around you.

God, thank you for your grace and forgiveness.

I forgive myself and release the burden of hurting others during my survival times.

ALPHA 16

PERCEPTION, PRESSURE, AND PERSEVERANCE

I'm somewhat impartial to these words because we all discern things from our level of understanding. Some discern from the surface; some discern in the spirit. And it's hard to teach people how to discern in the spirit because we are all navigating life at our own pace. This can feel crappy because perception can cause many to misinterpret the message. And then you find yourself trying to explain why? Because those that misinterpret can be so mean and hateful, which makes someone feel the pressure of needing to explain, and even in that, explaining can cause even more damage. People will hurt you because they are hurting; that hurt sometimes doesn't belong to you. That stuff can be attached so much that it has nothing to do with you, but the backlash can be tragic because you're present. I encourage you to read The Four Agreements and The Mastery of Love by Don Miguel Ruiz.

Embrace the reading. I promise you they are life-changing. This will help you persevere in times of persecution from broken people. Don't let the perception and pressure of broken people take you out. Just be intentional about being a good human. Only embrace what's next; remember, apologies are important, and the fruit is in forgiveness.

ALPHA 17

QUITTING

D on't be a quitter! Quitting is giving up

Why would you ever give up on yourself!

You are bigger than your circumstance.

Psalms 30:5

For his anger is but for a moment, and his favor is for a lifetime. Weeping may tarry for the night, but joy comes with the morning.

Psalm 16:11

You make known to me the path of life; in your presence, there is fullness of joy; at your right hand are pleasures forevermore. I ask that you wrap yourself tightly in God's word.

Hug yourself with scripture and hold on to his promise. Don't be distracted by what it feels like or even what it looks like. Aren't looks deceiving? Have you ever seen someone that you know on Instagram testiLYING? Ok, then, I promise you trouble doesn't last always. If no one has told you today that they love you, I love you, and I'm proud of you. Keep pushing. I promise you everything is going to be ok.

Father God, I come to you on behalf of this beautiful soul, reading the words you have given me. I ask that right now, in this very moment, allow your Holy Spirit to fill this space with your presence. Allow the comfort of your grace and mercy to be felt. Allow this reader to see who they are in the kingdom. Order their steps with your word. Show them that they are uniquely made in your image and that you have qualified them to journey this life. Show them that they are full of purpose. Let your unconditional love be felt beyond the feeling of despair. I decree and declare these things in Jesus 'mighty name, Amen.

ALPHA 18

REASONING AND REFLECTION

I rebuke the desire to reason and welcome reflection. Reasoning with yourself is finding a way to approve your mess.

Remember emotional manipulation. I came back to this because we will recreate a narrative and give it a different name. It's what we do as humans to give ourselves a pass on things that we know will not serve us well.

Stay in the mode of reflection so that you can always see yourself. Don't forget you're the only one to whom you cannot lie. It's true that you can begin to believe your very own lies. You will continue to harm yourself if you choose to deflect and resist the truth. Know this; this is self-work. No one needs to know, and those who will know will know on a need-to-know basis. When God gives you your wind to share, you do that. Until then, do the work, correct yourself, and make the adjustments so that you can align with God's will for you.

ALPHA 19

❦

SELF-SABOTAGE

That leads me to Self-Sabotage.

We are more responsible for the outcomes in our lives than we want to accept. It's so much easier to blame people and bad experiences and past situations for the things that happen to us in life. The truth is that how we rise when bad things happen will determine how life will go forward. We use tragedies as crutches. Excuses even. I do not deny that tragedy causes setbacks, but we cannot sit and waddle when bad things happen.

Alcoholism, drug addictions, and other toxic behaviors are typically birthed from trauma. Most of us become challenged with how to cope. How do we find our way out when things we don't understand happen? Ask God why is this happening to me?

Rest here and lean on his word. Please, lean not on your own understanding.

Romans 8:28

"And we know that God causes everything to work together for the good of those who love God and are called according to his purpose for them."

I know it can be challenging to make sense of things when tragedy strikes, but these are the uncontrollable occurrences He allows so we can reach for him and the comfort of his love.

Sometimes we seek comfort in people around us, but those people are also broken. That's why we need God. This is why he wants us to call on him so that he can prove to us that he is real!

Romans 10:13: For "everyone who calls on the name of the Lord will be saved."

All you have to do is call "Jesus," and he will answer. I'm a believer because he answered me.

I drank plenty of tequila and spent four years smoking a lot of weed unapologetically, but God's grace said, "I love you, girl, and you are uniquely made despite your foul language and your rump-shaking. You're my daughter. I didn't create you to be perfect. How else could I use you? That's why I say you are uniquely made!"

Thank you, Jesus!!!! HALLELUJAH FA-THER!!! WOOOOO, I PRAISE YOUR HOLY NAME!!! Even after writing this book, I know I will get it wrong again, and when I do, I know that your grace and mercy will be upon me and get me back in alignment with what you want me to accomplish. Thank you. If He's doing it for me, He's doing it for you!

ALPHA 20

TRIGGERED TEMPER

I feel like a triggered temper is more challenging to manage than someone with a bad temper. If you're anything like me and accepted that you have hosted or still have a bad temper and you've destroyed some things or possibly hurt some people when you were angry, I pray that you are aware now that you have learned to become a better manager of that beast. If you have ever gotten into trouble or damaged important relationships because of your inability to manage how you respond, I pray that you remain a work in progress and have found a way to tame yourself.

At one point, I wore rubber bands around my wrist because I was so eager to respond and GO OFF! I can give a tongue lashing like something you've never heard before. I've even been told I know how to split people in two, and they don't realize they've been torn a new one until they walk away and process. I guess that's the corporate cuss out.

What can become difficult to navigate is when you get to this point and you know better. You learn the importance of grace, mercy, forgiveness, boundaries, accountability, and unconditional love. Prioritizing and protecting your peace is critical, as well as managing self-love.

BUT PEOPLE SHOW UP NEEDING TO BE SLAPPED! Jesus, keep me! I'm going to make this quick.

Give God his children back! Let it be known how you desire to be treated! Stick to your agreements, be firm with how you wish to be treated, and if people can't treat you how you want to be treated, accept that they are not in season with whom you are becoming. It's ok to allow God to continue to do a mighty work in them. Have comfort in knowing that they are not your assignment. It's not your responsibility to enforce growth upon anyone. We are leaders; our job is to spread the good news of God's many divine works. We are messengers. Have you ever heard the saying, "you can lead the horse to the water, but you can't make him drink?" Welp, that's it, that's all, folks!

ALPHA 21

~

UNIQUE URGENCY

E verything I needed was already inside of me.

The spirit of God flows through me. The spirit of God is in all of us. When he calls you, you better answer. You will recognize his voice. His words will hug you and give you a sense of comfort like nothing you've ever felt. Ask him to increase your discernment. Ask him to guide you and make it plain. Ask him to show you the way. When I first heard the voice of God, I was 21 years old, and I just knew that I had it all under control. I knew my life would be different from that point on.

Little did I know he required so much more of me, more than I was ready to submit. It took over 20 years for me to hear his voice again. And although I haven't always made the best choices, he's never left me. He promised that he would never forsake me. He has indeed been a promise keeper. I now have the wisdom to know that those who are called will hear. I encourage you not to be afraid and to act with urgency. I told myself many years ago that when I heard his voice again, I would respond without delay. When I heard his sweet sovereign voice, I acted without delay. It is now my time to go forward. It is my time to receive and live the life my father wants me to live. No more suffering. This is where true abundance awaits. He wanted me to move my feet. I am blessed, and my success is inevitable. I now know that God has been preparing me for this very moment.

Therefore you, yes you…. It's your turn. Faith is an action word so trust him. I dare you to dream. And know this, if you are not fearful and nervous about the dream, it's not big enough. God wants to show you the miracle that you've been waiting for. He wants to show you that he has been your keeper and that you are not alone. Major favor is our portion; let's walk like we know! Let's show up as if it's already done. Claim it in the name of Jesus. Always be intentional about these three very important details.

1. Always welcome the Holy Spirit into your space; we serve a respectful God, and he can only enter where he is welcomed.

2. Lean not on your own understanding; always ask God to increase your discernment.

3. Ask God to guide you and keep you in alignment with the path he has paved for you.

4. Always give thanks. Acknowledge him in all things, even when it hurts. There's always a blessing in the storm and a Ram in the Bush!

5. Trust that God's love for us is unconditional and never failing as we journey; we will make mistakes, ask for forgiveness, and keep it pushing.

   Last but not least

6. Know that God is your BEST, BEST FRIEND you can just talk to him, host no shame, no guilt about anything. Remember, he wants you to give it to him. And although he is all-seeing and all-knowing, there is no better feeling than saying it to him yourself.

And don't make it all weird … If you are riding in your car talking to Jesus, don't be distracted by what may appear to be to others. Keep in mind that we live in a world where it's the law to operate a cell phone hands-free while driving. LOL

The time is NOW! Holy Spirit, Activate!

ALPHA 22

∼

VICTIM TO VICTOR

I am no longer a victim. I walk in victory. "Victory is mine," says the Lord.

And it is so…I've overcome. I'm more than a conqueror; I can do all things through Christ who strengthens me. I have to keep going. My commitment to God is to be a faithful servant - flawed and all. Someone needs my testimony. My life is valuable, and I will continue to do great things. I forgive myself and accept and release all things that no longer serve me. This is my winning season. I take back what the enemy tried to claim. My heavenly inheritance depends on my actions here on earth. I no longer lack. I don't live from check to check or favor to favor. God is the supplier of all my needs. When things happen that I cannot control, I will remain grateful and celebrate what I can't see.

I am a Winner!

ALPHA 23

WADDLING IN THE WOAH

I will no longer waddle in the Woah of life. I will grab ahold of tomorrow and make the best of every moment. I will seek the resources that I need to be better. I will be unashamed to ask for help. I will be intentional about asking God to increase my territory. Give me the strength to face my fears and know that you are with me to protect me and see me through it all. I will only dwell in places where I am celebrated.

I will see me. I will prioritize myself. I will speak life into myself. I will do things that make me happy. I will embrace healthy practices. I will respect my body when it tells me to rest. I will be gentle with myself. I will speak nicely to myself. I will say I love you and mean it.

I love you! - Me.

ALPHA 24

XENIC

I will no longer host illusions of who others told me I was. I will be who I am and be intentional about learning more about whom I want to be. I will level myself up and not play games with myself. I will no longer be whom I was told to be but be whom I desire to be unapologetically. I won't pretend to be a big deal because I am a big deal. I am enough; I don't need others to affirm me. I will no longer trauma bond. I will attract those that are healed and desire to sharpen me without a request. I will no longer betray myself. I will respect my boundaries and take charge of my life. Self-love and happiness are my mission, and I accept the task. I will not allow distractions to overtake me; I am ready for my overflow.

ALPHA 25

YOUNG

I'm ready to grow up spiritually; I'm prepared to embrace my grown-up posture. I release that damaged and traumatized child that has held me captive. I love you, young me, but I must let you go.

You are free to rest. You can trust that I got this!

I no longer need to keep company with my young self. The person I am today is bold and fearless and attracts reciprocating energy.

I have put my childish things aside.

1 Corinthians 13:11: When I was a child, I spake as a child, I understood as a child, I thought as a child: but when I became a man, I put away childish things.

ALPHA 26

ZANY

I will no longer conform and perform for others. I'm a leader, I will take charge, I'm a whole mood all by myself, I'm strong, I'm powerful, and I do not accept mediocrity from myself or others. I am medicine for the soul, and I bear fruit. I'm an asset, and I am important; what I have to say is valuable, and the generations today and those that will exist after I've passed away will live free because of me. I will be remembered, and my name will be relevant to many. I am powerful, baby! My presence is wanted and desired by those ready to step into their next!

FORWARD is MAJOR FAVOR! RISE UP and know this, even when you don't feel it, this read is proof positive that you are on the right road

Hell, I didn't know when I would finish this book, but I did it, and if I did it, I know you can do it!

Think Tall Thoughts, and if ya ass can't reach it, stand on the table!

Now, LETS GOOOOOOOO!

I LOVE YOU, AND THERE IS NOTHING YOU CAN EVER DO ABOUT IT!

I AM CHAVIS D. WALKER.

I AM THE COACH OF THE COURAGE.

AND I YIELD MY MIC!

ABOUT THE AUTHOR

Chavis D. Walker is a newly inspired author and a motivating and purpose-driven life coach. She is well known as The Coach of Courage and is an advocate for those who have been left to feel defeated. She has become the guru of helping others transition from victim to victor. She is well-traveled and loves to cook. She enjoys music of all genres and loves to dance. A true lover of nature, the beach gives her life.

After spending several years as a successful private practice dental and business consultant, she has boldly taken the leap of faith to embrace her anointing by surrendering to the word of God and encouraging others to live vibrantly and stand in their truth, accepting and releasing what no longer serves them.

Chavis, also known as Chaye, is currently working on her degree in Theology from Saint Leo University with the desire to become a Theology Professor. She holds an Associate in Psychology and minor studies in business management and finance. She has earned a holistic health and wellness certification with a primary focus and special studies on herbs and essential oils. She desires to free others from the post-trauma of old church hurt and judgment.

She became a registered wellness coach and yoga instructor with Yoga Alliance in 2017 and opened a Wellness Center in Georgia in 2018. She is currently working on opening a training facility in Florida called *The Synergy House Wellness Center*, formerly GotDammit Again.

Chavis is intentional about being an example of the unconditional love that the world needs. Unlearning and relearning how to withstand spiritual warfare is the key to living a victorious and abundant life. After all, it is a fixed fight.